RAT RACE NO MORE

How to Retire Early and Live Your Dreams

Mohd Faisal

Dedication:

To the Almighty God, whose unending mercy and unfailing direction enlighten our pathways and give us the courage to achieve our aspirations,

And to you, dear reader, who holds the key to your own future in your hands,

May the words of "Rat Race No More: How to Retire Early and Live Your Dreams" serve as a guiding light for you as you strive for financial independence and a fulfilling life.

May you escape the grip of the never-ending rat race with confidence in the divine and tenacity in your heart, and move into a future where your ambitions are not just aspirations but your everyday realities.

This book is committed to the idea that you can retire early and actually lead the life you've always wanted provided you have faith, tenacity, and the appropriate information.

May you have a happy trip and realize all of your aspirations.
Thankful and hopeful

~Mohd Faisal

"If you don't find a way to make money while you sleep, you will work until you die."

- WARREN BUFFETT

CONTENTS

INTRODUCTION

Many of us are caught in the rat race, a continuous loop driven by the unrelenting chase of riches and prestige. We struggle through traffic, get up early, work long hours at jobs that frequently don't seem meaningful, and then we come home fatigued with little energy or time left to pursue our interests and aspirations. It's a cycle that appears impossible to break, a maze we can't help but navigate every day and every year.

What if, though, there was a way out? What if you could leave the rat race behind and take control of your life by retiring early? Imagine being able to pursue your goals, go on adventures, spend more time with loved ones, and do the things that genuinely make you happy.

In "Rat Race No More: How to Retire Early and Live Your Dreams," we look at the options and methods that can release you from the grind and give you control over your financial destiny. This book serves as a road map for creating a life that is in line with your beliefs and passions, as well as a manual for turning your aspirations into reality.

The ideas of financial independence and early retirement will be covered in detail in the pages that follow, along with tried-and-true methods for prudent money management, saving, and investing. We'll also look into the experiences of those who have managed to flee the rat race and are now leading independent lives. Your own path to freedom will be inspired by and guided by their experiences.

"Rat Race No More" provides helpful guidance, doable actions, and a new perspective on what it means to achieve financial independence and retire early, regardless of where you are in your career—whether you're just getting started, in the middle of the rat race, or getting close to retirement age. Stop going around in circles and begin living the life you've always wanted. Welcome to the journey toward a day when the rat race is a thing of the past and you may live the life of your dreams.

CHAPTER 1: ESCAPING THE RAT RACE

1.1 The Rat Race Defined

Ah, the notorious Rat Race—that never-ending hamster wheel that is life! Let's go right into this ridiculous carnival that is our professions, shall we?

Imagine this: Your alarm clock screams in your ear, waking you up and bringing with it the start of another exciting day in the Rat Race. You drag yourself out of bed, don your business attire, and slog through traffic to get to your desk, where you'll spend the next eight hours performing a job you might not even recall applying for. Sounds recognizable?

Let's define the Rat Race right now. It's that elaborate ruse where you trade the most enjoyable parts of your day for a wage that is only sufficient to keep the lights on and feed your caffeine addiction. Your supervisor probably believes your name is "Hey, you!" since you're not following dreams; instead, you're chasing deadlines.

However, there's still more! A hefty helping of soul-crushing meetings, mind-numbing duties, and an insatiable thirst for your valuable time are all part of the Rat Race. Work, consume, repeat is a never-ending cycle that is frequently broken by the dreaded Sunday night blues as you think about another week of this craziness.

Define the Rat Race, then, why? Because the first step to escaping is realizing how silly it all is. This chapter exists to empower you, not to make fun of you. You can arrange your escape by equipping yourself with the information necessary by realizing what the Rat Race really is. It's time to put your aspirations and interests front and center in your life and wave goodbye to that wheel.

Please fasten your seatbelt because we are going to reveal this Rat Race for the circus that it is, and together we will discover the exit.

1.2 The Consequences Of A Traditional Career

The effects of a traditional career, ah, absolutely. Please allow me to relate a little personal story in this deliciously sarcastic style.

You see, I used to be caught in the shackles of a traditional career. My daily routine was about as fascinating as watching paint dry, and my job title was longer than my attention span in office meetings. It did, however, have some great bonuses, such as a cubicle with a view of the vending machine. Really impressive, no?

Let's now discuss the results, shall we? Imagine this: You carefully work your way up the corporate ladder for years. When you eventually reach the top, you discover that the ladder was positioned against the incorrect wall the entire time! You've earned the golden handcuffs, congrats! Although you are now making more money than you could have ever imagined, you are working so much that you hardly have any free time.

Not to mention the advantages of a traditional profession for your health. Who needs a gym subscription when you can experience heart palpitations brought on by stress? They claim that the never-ending deadlines, workplace politics, and soul-crushing meetings are the key components of a heart-healthy lifestyle.

However, there's still more! Traditional occupations are accompanied by "commute rage." All this simply to go to a location you'd rather not be, spending hours in traffic and wondering what the point of life is while snarled up on the highway. With ergonomic seats and artificial lights, it is the contemporary equivalent of a daily torture chamber.

I don't want to present a picture that is too gloomy, but it is important to understand these repercussions. After all, it was my own experience with the traditional job route that motivated me to look for a more meaningful and liberated way of life. So, dear reader, keep in mind that there is a world beyond the cubicle and a life outside of the nine to five. In the chapters that follow, we'll look at ways to escape these funny yet constricting effects and enjoy life on your own terms.

1.3 The Early Retirement Dream

Oh, let's discuss the dream of early retirement, shall we? Imagine this: While the rest of the world is caught in rush hour traffic, frantically trying to get to their cubicles, you are relaxing on a spotless beach, drinking a coconut under a little umbrella. Right, that sounds like a dream. It's not quite as unbelievable as you may assume.

The early retirement dream is the unicorn of adulthood and the stuff of legends. It's the alluring thought of leaving the Rat Race much before society tells you to. It's about accepting a life of freedom, adventure, and pleasure and taking charge of your financial future.

However, why wait until you're wrinkled and gray to enjoy life to the fullest? I'm not advocating that you retire at the lovely old age of 25 (unless, of course, that's your thing). Imagine having the time and financial stability to follow your hobbies while still waking up each day with a feeling of purpose and doing what you love.

The Early Retirement Dream is not simply a fun vision, though; it is actually a well-thought-out, calculated way of living. To create a retirement that is more like an extended vacation, one must actively save, make sensible investments, and make deliberate decisions.

I'll be honest about it now. This desire requires commitment and determination to realize. It necessitates reassessing your priorities, challenging social conventions, and maybe shrinking your life. You'll understand that it was all worthwhile when you start to watch your retirement fund increase and your aspirations become a little bit more true.

So, dear reader, we'll go more deeply into the complexities of the Early Retirement Dream in this chapter. We'll look at the procedures, tactics, and mental adjustments required to make your goal a reality for you. After all, why just imagine an early retirement when you can actually experience it?

1.4 Setting Your Retirement Goals

Setting retirement objectives is like to choosing the ice cream flavors you'll eat when you're a hundred years old, isn't it? But hey, bear with me while we discuss this.

So there I was, daydreaming about the time when I would finally be retired and could spend my days playing golf, traveling, or doing anything else I pleased. But hold on, you don't automatically become retired if your birthday cake has had a particular number of candles blown out. Plan beforehand, please. You need objectives!

Setting retirement objectives is similar to making your own personal bucket list for future decades. It involves imagining your life after being freed from the desk, the deadlines, and the obligations of your traditional work.

Do you imagine yourself enjoying an espresso in a sleepy Italian town, for example? Maybe you enjoy climbing the Inca Trail to Machu Picchu more? Maybe all you want is guilt-free access to binge-watching your favorite TV episodes. Your retirement plans should be as individual as your nightwear, whatever they may be.

The trick, though, is this Retirement objectives require strategy as well as aspiration. How much cash will you need to achieve those objectives? Do you have a target retirement age in mind? Will you choose for full-time leisure or stick with your flexible part-time job?

Imagine that you have a penchant for gathering valuable antique action figures. You'll need to calculate how many of those miniature plastic heroes you can purchase without going bankrupt. Setting precise, doable, and, dare I say, little ludicrously ambitious retirement objectives becomes important in this situation.

CHAPTER 2: FINANCIAL FOUNDATIONS

2.1 Creating A Budget That Works

Let's dive into the exciting world of budgeting, shall we? Prepare for a wild trip as you enter the world of spreadsheets, calculators, and financial responsibilities.

Consider this now: You make the decision to take charge of your financial future. You're sick of seeing your money go more quickly than a tray of cookies at a kid's birthday celebration. What do you do then? You put forth the effort to make a budget that is effective.

Setting limits for a spendthrift child is similar to creating a budget. It involves dictating where your money may and cannot go. Fear not, though; it's not as limiting as it seems.

Consider that you enjoy specialty coffee. Instead of giving the barista at your preferred coffee shop your whole salary, a budget enables you to establish a limit on your coffee expenditures while still enjoying the odd cappuccino. Finding the ideal balance between self-care and financial restraint is important.

Oh, but the budgetary fun don't end there! You may track your expenditure with the aid of a well-made budget, find areas where you can make savings, and earmark money for retirement aspirations. It's like to having a financial GPS that directs you to your desired locations.

The real kicker is that your spending plan should reflect your personal musical preferences. It is a customised road plan that considers your earnings, outgoings, and financial objectives. Your budget should support your goals, whether they be early retirement, a global tour, or a collection of rare action figures (yes, we still have them).

2.2 Eliminating Debt And Building Savings

Ah, the delightful music of financial independence! This chapter will cover the thrilling process of paying off debt and increasing your savings. You'll feel as if you're on a rollercoaster without the sickness, I promise.

Debt cancellation:

Let's speak about the financial monster that prowls about in your closet. It's time to kill the debt beast, whether it's a credit card balance, school debts, or that terrible impulse buy of a giant garden gnome.

Let's use an illustration where you have high-interest credit card debt. Make an active plan to reduce the balance instead of just paying the minimal amount due and seeing the balance scarcely change. You'll be astounded by how rapidly that debt disappears if you devote a sizable amount of your salary to paying it off.

Advice on Getting Out of Debt:

Choose a debt-reduction plan that works for you, such as the snowball or avalanche methods. While the avalanche technique starts with high-interest debt, the snowball method prioritizes paying down the lowest debt. Choose the one that inspires you the most.

Cut Wasteful expenditure:

Determine where you can reduce your expenditure. Refrain from making impulse purchases, cancel unneeded subscriptions, and prepare meals at home more frequently.

Increase Your Income:

To temporarily increase your income, think about picking up side jobs or contracting work. Every additional dollar you make can be used to pay off debt.

Investing Savings:

Let's now switch to accumulating those savings. You will be grateful for this in the future.

Think about investing a portion of your monthly salary into a high-yield savings account or a stock portfolio. Over time, that money increases, and you may use it to finance your desired impromptu getaways or your ideal retirement.

Building Savings: Some Advice

Clarify Your Objectives: Specify your financial objectives. How much do you want to set up for retirement, unanticipated expenses, or that ideal getaway? You stay motivated if you have clear goals.

Automate Savings: Set up automatic withdrawals from your checking account for investment or savings purposes. Think of your savings as a recurring, non-negotiable bill.

Start by establishing an emergency fund to pay for unforeseen costs. At least three to six months' worth of costs for living should be kept in an account that is easy to access.

When you have an emergency fund in place, think carefully about investing your remaining funds in securities such as stocks, bonds, or real estate. Compared to a traditional savings account, investments offer the potential to increase your wealth more quickly.

The path to financial freedom is a marathon, not a sprint, so keep that in mind. By getting rid of debt and increasing your savings, you're taking crucial steps to protecting your future and realizing your retirement goals.

2.3 Putting Money Into The Future

Let's now explore the fascinating realm of future investment! It's like using your money to play a game of strategy, and the results may be thrilling.

How to Invest:

Think of your money like a skilled young acrobat who does flips and somersaults to multiply. Investing accomplishes this by assisting your money to increase throughout time. This is why it's crucial:

Consider investing in a diverse portfolio of equities as an example. Your investment increased over time along with the success and growth of those businesses. While enjoying your favorite beverage, you saw your money performing a financial medley.

Investing Advice:

1. **Start Early:** In the world of investment, time is your best friend. Your money has more time to grow the earlier you start. Over time, even modest investments made regularly can provide large returns.

2. **Diversify Your Portfolio:** Avoid putting all of your financial eggs in one basket. Invest in a variety of asset types, including equities, bonds, real estate, and even atypical forms of investing like cryptocurrency.

3. **Take into account risk tolerance:** Find out how much risk you can take. Do you feel comfortable investing in the stock market despite its probable ups and downs, or do you favor more cautious strategies? Your investing decisions should be influenced by your risk tolerance.

4. **Seek Professional Advice:** Consult a financial counselor if you're unclear of where to invest or how to build a diverse portfolio. They may assist in adjusting an investing plan to fit your objectives and risk tolerance.

Make consistent contributions to your investing accounts. This is number five. Dollar-cost averaging is a technique that lessens the effect of market volatility on your assets.

6. **The long view:** Investing is not a get-rich-quick plan. It's a lengthy project. During market gyrations, resist the desire to panic and maintain attention on your financial objectives.

Investment Types:

There are several investing alternatives available. Here are a few illustrations:

Stocks: Due to market volatility and the potential for big gains, investing in individual business shares carries a higher risk.

Bonds: Bonds are a more conservative investment choice since they are seen as being safer than stocks and yield a consistent interest payment.

Mutual Funds: These funds combine the funds of several individuals to make investments in a broad portfolio of stocks, bonds, and other assets.

Real Estate: Real estate investments, such as those in rental homes or real estate investment trusts (REITs), can yield rental income as well as possible capital growth.

Retirement plans: To maximize tax advantages while saving for retirement, contribute as much as possible to tax-advantaged retirement plans like 401(k)s and IRAs.

Keep in mind that investing is a journey that calls for knowledge and perseverance. The correct plan and a well-diversified portfolio can help you position yourself for financial security and get closer to your long-held goals of early retirement. Put your financial thinking cap on and let's start making those investments!

2.4 Understanding The Power Of Compounding

Gather around, ladies and gentlemen, as we are about to go off on a heroic expedition to discover the mystifying and enchanted Power of Compounding! It's like watching an endless magic show with your money.

Compounding: What Is It?

Compounding is a phenomena in which the interest or returns generated by your money are used to increase its value. To put it another way, imagine a snowball rolling down a hill, gathering more snow as it goes, and expanding and speeding up with each spin.

Consider investing $1,000 in a fund that offers an 8% yearly return. You will accrue interest of $80 in the first year. But the magic is here: You will receive interest on both your initial $1,000 investment and the $80 you made in the first year in the second year. As a result of compounding, you make $80 plus a little bit more. This snowball effect might cause your original investment to grow substantially over time.

Utilizing Compounding: Some Advice

Start Early:

Getting a head start is essential for optimizing compounding's benefits. Even modest investments made in your early years have the potential to become large sums of money over time.

Make consistent contributions to your assets because consistency is king. Investments made on a regular basis add to the snowball effect.

Dividends and interest generated by your assets should be reinvested as opposed to being cashed out. This enables your money to expand farther.

Compounding takes time, so don't anticipate benefits right away. Patience is a virtue. Be patient and wait for your investments to pay off.

Profit from Tax-Deferred Accounts: Use tax-advantaged accounts like 401(k)s and IRAs to save your money so that it can grow tax-free or tax-deferred, maximizing the power of compounding.

Compounding Frequency: Your assets will increase more quickly if they compound more regularly. Search for investments with more frequent compounding of returns, such as monthly or quarterly.

Long-Term Advantages

Long-term advantages of compounding are what truly make it beautiful. The growth of your investments gets more significant with time. It is comparable to sowing a financial seed and then witnessing it blossom into a massive oak tree. When the time comes to enjoy the shade, your financial tree will be larger the earlier you sow that seed.

So, dear reader, whether you're saving for retirement, a fantasy vacation, or your very own action figure collection, knowing and utilizing the power of compounding may help you achieve your financial objectives in a more realistic and, dare I say, magical way.

CHAPTER 3: ALTERNATIVE INCOME STREAMS

Investigating Sources Of Passive Income

How Does Passive Income Work?

You may make money with little to no active effort if you have passive income. It's not dependent on exchanging your time for money, and it may come from a variety of places. Consider it your safety net for money and a pass to your early retirement goals.

Consider owning rental homes as an example. Without having to put in daily labor as a landlord, you may receive rent every month. Or you may buy equities that pay dividends, and those businesses will reward you with consistent dividend payments.

Passive income in action would be that.

Different Sources of Passive Income:

Property rentals: Owning real estate and receiving rental income is a prime example of passive income.

Stocks that pay monthly dividends: By purchasing shares of companies that do this, you may share in their profits.

Through peer-to-peer lending systems, you may lend money to people or small businesses while still earning interest.

Royalties: If you're a creative, you may be able to profit from royalties associated with music, patents, books, and other forms of intellectual property.

Real estate investment trusts, or REITs, are comparable to mutual funds for real estate. Dividends from a diverse portfolio of properties will be paid to you if you invest in REITs.

Affiliate marketing is a way to advertise goods or services online and get paid a fee for each lead or sale that results from your recommendations.

Guidelines for Investigating Passive Income Sources:

Diversify: Don't place all of your eggs in one type of passive income. Spread risk by varying the sources of your income.

Research and education: Before taking the plunge, fully grasp the risks and benefits associated with each passive income choice. Think about reading books, enrolling in classes, or consulting with professionals.

Initial Effort: A lot of passive income sources need upfront work, including starting a business or buying rental properties. Once established, they are able to exhibit true passivity.

Maintenance: Although it may be little compared to a full-time work, certain passive income streams may need to be managed or maintained on occasion.

Long-Term Perspective: Be patient since it takes time to develop sizable passive income. They can offer financial security and flexibility as your revenue streams increase.

Always keep in mind that passive income is not a get-rich-quick program. It's a long-term plan that can greatly improve your financial situation and move you closer to realizing your early retirement goal. In order to reap the rewards of your financial effort, examine the options, select the ones that are consistent with your goals, and then let those income streams flow.

3.2 Freelancing And Side Hustles

Ah, the world of freelancing and side jobs, where you may pursue your interests and abilities as businesses on your own terms. As if you could have your financial cake and eat it too!

Freelancing:

Being a freelancer is similar to being a digital nomad in the workplace. You don't have to work a 9 to 5 job since you may provide your talents and services to customers or businesses. Since it may be done remotely, you can complete it from any location with an internet connection.

Let's take an example where you have a talent for graphic design. Both corporations and private clients can use your design skills. You select your clients, establish your own pricing, and work on the things you're passionate about. Even if it's work, it's work you can control.

Side Hustles:

A side business is like moonlighting for money and pleasure. Along with your normal career, you explore these other sources of money. They might be anything from providing advisory services to online handcrafted artisan sales.

Say, for example, that you are an expert at restoring old bicycles in addition to being a teacher by day. You spend your weekends repairing used bikes and selling them for a healthy profit. That is a side business that may help you bolster your financial situation.

Advice for Side Jobs and Freelancing:

1. Identify Your Skills: Determine what abilities or skills you have that are marketable. Writing, graphic design, computing, cooking, or even playing an instrument are all examples of creative endeavors.

2. *Promote Yourself:* Establish an online identity to highlight your abilities. Promote your services on social media, online portfolios, and freelancing websites to draw in clients or consumers.

3. *Set Clear Goals:* Specify your financial objectives for your freelance work or side business. Are you doing it to reduce debt, fund a trip, or increase your retirement account?

4. *Time management:* Coordinate your primary employment, side business, and personal obligations. Burnout may be avoided by practicing effective time management.

5. *Legal and Tax Considerations:* Be aware of the financial and legal ramifications of your side business or freelance employment. It could entail registering a firm, paying taxes, or adhering to particular rules.

6. *Customer Service:* Provide outstanding customer service to have a good reputation. A satisfied client or customer is more likely to recommend you to others.

Dreams of financial independence and an early retirement might be realized through side jobs and freelancing. They provide freedom, the prospect for additional money, and the chance to follow your hobbies.

These alternative income streams might be your key to achieving financial independence on your terms, whether your goal is to leave the traditional 9-to-5 job or just increase your savings.

In order to start freelancing or starting a side business, start thinking about your abilities and hobbies.

3.3 Real Estate Investments

Why Real Estate?
For generations, people have preferred real estate as an investment, and for good reason. It provides various sources of income, the chance for property appreciation, and tax advantages. Here are some reasons why buying real estate is a common decision:

As an illustration, consider buying a rental property. Rent from your renters pays your mortgage and other monthly expenditures. You benefit from both property appreciation and rental revenue as the value of the property rises over time. Win-win situation!

Real estate investment strategies:

Residential or commercial properties can be purchased as rentals and rented to tenants.

Invest in shares of businesses that own and manage properties that generate revenue by using real estate investment trusts (REITs).

Real estate crowdfunding involves combining your funds with those of other investors to invest in real estate projects.

Advice on Investing in Real Estate:

Location, Location, Location: Before making an investment, do your homework on the area. Take into account elements including neighborhood attractiveness, demographic trends, and job growth.

Calculate your budget, taking into account the purchase price, ongoing maintenance expenses, and prospective rental revenue. Obtain funding via mortgages or other methods.

Decide if you'll manage the property yourself or if you'll contract with a property management firm. Although management might be time-consuming, it is necessary to preserve the value of the property and guarantee tenant happiness.

Don't concentrate all of your real estate investments on a single area, neighborhood, or market. Increase portfolio diversity to reduce risk.

Recognize Market Cycles: There are cycles of growth and decrease in the real estate market. You can choose investments wisely if you are aware of these cycles.

Legal and tax considerations: Comply with local laws and be aware of how your real estate investments may affect your taxes.

Long-Term View: Real estate investments frequently provide their greatest long-term returns. Be patient and refrain from forming snap judgments based on transient market movements.

Potential advantages:

Real estate investments may provide the following advantages:

Rental revenue can offer a consistent stream of financial flow.

Appreciation: Over time, properties frequently gain value.

Tax Benefits: Mortgage interest, property depreciation, and other tax benefits are available to real estate investors.

Diversification: Adding real estate to your financial portfolio might be beneficial.

Leverage: By using loans to buy properties, you might increase your profits.

Therefore, the world of real estate investments provides a plethora of alternatives to increase your income and get closer to your goals of early retirement, whether you're thinking about renting out your property, investing in REITs, or investigating real estate crowdfunding. Time to don your real estate investor hat and begin expanding your portfolio of properties!

3.4 The Gig Economy And Online Business

Gig Economy

People who operate in the gig economy frequently freelance or on a project basis for several clients. You may pick when, where, and how you work in this flexible world.

Imagine you have a talent for graphic design. On websites like Upwork or Fiverr, you may advertise your design services and accept jobs from people all around the world. You create a portfolio of pleased clients while working on your own terms.

Online Commerce:

Online companies are digital enterprises that make money through online services, digital goods, or e-commerce. They may be extremely profitable and perhaps appeal to a worldwide audience.

Consider this scenario: You have a deep interest for old vinyl recordings. You make the decision to launch an internet store where you offer collectors rare vinyl recordings. Your online business succeeds if it has an e-commerce website and a successful marketing plan.

Advice for Online Businesses and the Gig Economy:

Choose a specialization that fits with your abilities, hobbies, and market need. The better, the more specialized.

Promote Yourself: Whether you run an internet business or work as a freelancer, good marketing is essential. Create a solid online presence through e-commerce platforms, social media, or a website.

Customer satisfaction: Your reputation is crucial in the gig economy. To establish a solid reputation and draw in recurring customers, provide high-quality work and offer great customer service.

Online Business Strategy: Have a detailed business strategy if you're operating an online business. Recognize your target market, rivals, and revenue generation strategy.

Maintain a record of your earnings and outgoing costs. Think about opening a different bank account just for your business or freelancing revenue.

Scaling: Look at ways to grow your company or your freelancing work. Can you increase the number of items you sell, grow your clientele, or automate certain tasks?

Potential advantages

Flexibility: In the gig economy, you may choose the tasks that interest you and work at your own pace.

Global Reach: By connecting with clients on a global scale, online firms may increase their market and revenue potential.

Low Overhead: Compared to traditional brick-and-mortar enterprises, starting up many internet firms and freelancing employment is quite inexpensive.

Multiple Income Streams: You may diversify your income in the gig economy by taking on a number of jobs or projects at once.

Passion and Creativity: You may frequently transform your interests and skills into a source of money through online enterprises.

These alternative revenue streams provide enormous potential for financial development and flexibility, whether you're exploring the Gig Economy as a freelancer or delving into the world of internet business. It's time to use your talents and entrepreneurial spirit to take advantage of the digital economy and make your long-held early retirement goals a reality.

CHAPTER 4: ACHIEVING FINANCIAL INDEPENDENCE

4.1 Calculating Your Financial Independence Number

It's time to play the numbers game, and this isn't bingo; it's your route to financial freedom, ladies and gents! This chapter will go in-depth on the crucial process of determining your Financial Independence Number (FIN).

How Do I Calculate My Financial Independence Number (FIN)?

The sum of money you need to reach financial independence is symbolized by your FIN, a mysterious number. It is the treasure box that, once full, enables you to retire early and lead a life that suits you.

Take $50,000 as an example of your yearly costs. In this scenario, calculating your yearly costs by the amount of years you hope to be financially independent yields your FIN. Your FIN would be $50,000 x 30 = $1.5 million if your goal is to retire early and live in financial freedom for 30 years.

Tips for Figuring Out Your FIN:

1. Choose the Lifestyle You Want: Start by picturing the retirement you've always wanted. What are the likely costs you'll have in retirement? Be practical, but also keep in mind the things you wish to do and encounter.

2. Account for Inflation: Take inflation into account while determining your FIN. Your costs will probably rise as the buying value of money declines over time.

3. Emergency Fund: Ensure that your FIN has a reserve set up to handle unforeseen costs.

4. Healthcare Costs: Remember to budget for probable medical expenditures as well as insurance payments.

5. Debt Considerations: Include the cost of repaying any existing debts in your annual costs.

6. Expected Investment Returns: Take into account the anticipated rates of return on your assets. A well-diversified investment portfolio can offer a reliable income source in retirement.

7. *Contingency:* Create a cushion in your FIN to take into consideration unforeseen costs or market volatility.

The 4% Rule's Influential Effects:

The 4% rule is one often applied generalization. According to this theory, if you take 4% of your investment portfolio each year while you're retired, your funds should survive for at least 30 years. If your FIN, for instance, is $1.5 million, you might withdraw $60,000 every year (4% of $1.5 million) to pay for costs.

It's crucial to keep in mind that this rule should only be used as a general guideline and not as a firm promise. The sustainability of your portfolio might be impacted by market changes and unique situations.

A critical step on your path to early retirement is figuring out your Financial Independence Number. It aids in the planning of your savings and investment plans and gives you a specific financial objective to strive for. With the help of your FIN, you can take decisive action to make your aspirations of an early retirement a reality. The earlier you begin, the nearer you will be to that elusive number. Grab a cup of coffee and your calculator, and let's start adding those numbers up!

4.2 Smart Investment And Savings Techniques

It's like creating your own financial masterpiece when you save properly and invest smartly, so welcome! This chapter will look at wealth-building tactics that can help you get to your Financial Independence Number (FIN).

Savings Methods:

Automate Savings: Set up automatic withdrawals from your checking account for investment or savings purposes. Consider saving as a monthly expense that cannot be waived.

Budgeting: Establish a budget that supports your financial objectives. Track your spending, look for places where you can decrease costs, and set aside money for investments and savings.

Create an emergency fund to take care of unforeseen costs. At least three to six months' worth of costs for living should be kept in an account that is easy to access.

Debt management tip: Pay off high-interest obligations first. You may free up money by paying off debt, which also saves you money on interest and allows you to save and invest more.

Investing Methods

Differing asset types, such as equities, bonds, real estate, and alternative assets, should be represented in your investing portfolio to provide diversification. Risk is spread via diversification.

Asset Allocation: Select the appropriate mixture of assets depending on your risk appetite and financial objectives. Generally speaking, younger investors can afford to take more risks, whereas those who are getting close to retirement could choose a more cautious strategy.

Consistent Contributions: Whether it's a retirement account, brokerage account, or other investment vehicle, make consistent contributions to your investment accounts.

Long-Term View: Investing is a long-term process. Put off making snap judgments based on momentary market changes.

Maximize your contributions to tax-advantaged retirement plans such as 401(k)s and IRAs. These accounts have tax advantages and can hasten the growth of your money.

Additional Approaches

Reduce Expenses: Constantly search for methods to cut back on wasteful spending in your everyday life. Every dollar that is saved can be invested.

Consider seeing a financial counselor to create a customized savings and investment strategy. Seek Professional Advice. Based on your particular financial position, a specialist can offer advice.

Keep Up: Keep abreast on market developments and financial news. Making wise investing selections requires knowledge, which is power.

Review and Modify: Regularly evaluate your financial objectives, portfolio, and strategy. Your financial strategy has to be adjusted when your life circumstances change.

Keep in mind that achieving financial independence requires

patience and perseverance, not a sprint. Your allies will be discipline, consistency, and a dedication to your financial objectives. You're not only getting closer to your FIN by saving and investing sensibly, but you're also ensuring a better financial future for yourself and your loved ones. Accept these tactics, continue on your path, and let the miracle of compounding work its magic for you.

4.3 Building Multiple Income Streams

Why Have Multiple Streams of Income?

Diversifying your sources of income can act as a financial trampoline that can help you achieve your early retirement goals rather than merely as a safety net. This is why it's essential:

Consider the following scenario: You work a full-time job, but you also profit from investments and a side business. The other revenue sources might assist in keeping you afloat if one suffers a loss. It's similar to your financial house being supported by several pillars.

Multiple income stream types include:

1. Your primary source of income, usually a full-time employment, is your primary job.

2. A part-time employment or business that provides additional revenue in addition to your main work is referred to as a "side hustle."

3. *Investments:* Earnings from investments, including capital

gains, dividends, and interest.

4. *Passive revenue:* Earnings produced with little or no work, such as through royalties, affiliate marketing, or rental revenue.

5. *Freelancing:* Additional income from consulting or freelancing work on top of your normal salary.

How to Create Multiple Income Streams:

1. *Identify possibilities:* To find prospective side jobs or freelancing possibilities, think about your talents, hobbies, and passions.

2. *Time Management:* Use your time wisely to balance several sources of income. Set timetables, prioritize chores, and stay away from burnout.

3. *Financial Goals:* Align each source of income with definite financial objectives, such as eliminating debt, setting aside money for retirement, or taking a long-awaited vacation.

4. To spread risk, diversify your sources of income. Do not rely on a single source of income.

5. *Tax Considerations:* Recognize how your revenue sources will affect your taxes. For advice, speak with a tax expert.

6. Emergency Fund: Keep an emergency fund on hand to meet unforeseen costs or changes in income.

Benefits of Having Several Income Streams:

Increased Financial Security: Having many sources of income offers a safety net in times of financial difficulty.

Faster Financial Goals: Having more money might help you reach other financial objectives, such as early retirement.

Flexibility: Having many sources of income gives you the freedom to adjust to a variety of conditions.

Reduced Dependence: Your reliance on a single source of income decreases, easing your financial strain.

Personal Growth: Having numerous sources of income can help you grow personally and professionally as you take advantage of new chances.

It's not about working longer hours; it's about working smarter and developing financial stability. It's similar to putting together a toolbox for money, with different tools for different jobs. By diversifying your sources of income, you increase your chances of achieving your early retirement goals while also securing your financial future. Start looking into potential sources of income, accept diversity, and watch your money grow!

4.4 Protecting Your Financial Future

We're now moving into the area of financial guardianship, where you take on the role of defender of your arduously acquired money. Consider this as your financial equivalent of a coat of armor, protecting you from any unforeseen difficulties life may present.

Why Should You Secure Your Financial Future?

Life has a way of throwing curveballs at you when you're actively striving toward financial freedom. Your financial stability may be threatened by unexpected illnesses, mishaps, or economic downturns. Because of this, protecting your wealth is not just a good idea but also a need.

Consider the following scenario: You are on the verge of achieving your objective of early retirement when a significant medical expenditure strikes you like a freight train. You will have a financial shield to withstand these storms if you have adequate financial protection.

Guidelines for Financial Future Protection:

Maintain a reserve of at least three to six months' worth of living expenditures in case of emergencies. Your safety net is provided by this cash cushion in case unplanned costs emerge.

Insurance: Make an investment in complete insurance protection. This covers property insurance to preserve your possessions, life insurance to ensure the financial security of your family, disability insurance to safeguard your income, and health insurance to pay for medical expenses.

Organize your estate such that it contains a will, a power of attorney, and a healthcare directive. Estate planning reduces the complexity of the legal process and guarantees that your assets are dispersed in accordance with your preferences.

Consider using legal measures to preserve your assets, such as creating trusts or limited liability organizations (LLCs). By taking these precautions, you can protect your wealth against prospective debtors and legal troubles.

Regular Review: Review and update your estate plan, insurance policies, and financial strategy on a regular basis. Your protection tactics should adapt as your life circumstances do.

Spend some time educating yourself on the dangers and difficulties associated with money. It's crucial to comprehend the tiny print of investment contracts and insurance policies.

Prevent Overleveraging: Be wary about taking on too much debt. Your financial stability may be seriously at danger if you have a lot of debt.

Investment Portfolio Diversification: To lower risk, diversify your investment holdings. A single investment or asset type should not include all of your assets.

Future *Perspective*

To preserve your financial future, keep in mind that you must take a long-term view in addition to possessing the appropriate insurance policies and legal documentation. It involves making sure that your wealth can endure life's unforeseen difficulties and sustain your early retirement aspirations even in the face of hardship.

By putting these safety measures into place, you're building a financial wall that will give you peace of mind as you face life's difficulties. Always bear in mind that securing your financial future is a crucial component of your journey as you get closer to your Financial Independence Number (FIN). Take these actions seriously and use your financial stability as the foundation for your early retirement aspirations.

CHAPTER 5: CRAFTING YOUR EARLY RETIREMENT LIFESTYLE

5.1 Defining Your Retirement Dreams

Why Define Your Dreams for Retirement?

Retirement is about welcoming a life that you've created and imagined, not merely saying goodbye to your employment. You may give your financial journey purpose and direction by outlining your retirement aspirations.

Imagine that you've always wanted to travel the globe, give back to a cause you care about, or spend more time with your loved ones. These aspirations become the compass for your retirement strategy.

How to Identify Your Retirement Dreams:

Consider Your Passions: What pursuits, pastimes, or issues fuel your passion? Consider what actually brings you joy.

Travel and adventure: Think about the places you've always yearned to see. Do you fantasize of taking a cross-country road trip, seeing several Mediterranean islands, or experiencing various cultures?

Preferences in lifestyle: Imagine the ideal day in your life. Do you favor living in the city, the calm countryside, or somewhere in between?

Think about your connections with your family and friends. How do you plan to spend your free time in retirement with loved ones?

Personal Development: Consider your potential for improvement. Retirement might be a time to explore new interests, enroll in classes, or even launch a new venture.

Giving Back: Think about if you want to volunteer or participate in charity. The opportunity to change your town or the globe after retirement can provide you the time and resources you need.

Health and Well-Being: Pay attention to your emotional and psychological health. How will you maintain a healthy, active lifestyle in retirement?

Planning Your Retirement:

Start developing your retirement vision after giving your dreams some thought. Use any creative method that speaks to you, whether it be writing it down or making vision boards. Your financial and lifestyle choices will be guided by your vision.

Financial Coordination:

You must match your financial strategy with your long-term goals after outlining your retirement aspirations. Determine how much money you'll need to support your preferred standard of living in retirement. This phase is essential because it gives you something concrete to strive for.

Keep in mind that your retirement goals are particular to you. They serve as your North Star, pointing you in the direction of a meaningful, contented retirement that is in line with your most cherished goals. So, use your imagination to its fullest, be very clear about what your aspirations are, and allow them guide you on your financial path to the early retirement you've always wanted.

5.2 Location Independence And Travel

We're about to explore the fascinating world of location freedom and travel during your early retirement, so grab your luggage and passport. It's like having access to an endless playground!

Why Value Travel and Location Independence?

The ability to travel and live independently are two of the most prized benefits of early retirement. Many people wish they could travel and see other cultures and countries without being confined to a desk.

Consider, for instance, waking up to the tranquil splendor of the Swiss Alps, wandering through the remains of the Roman Empire, or enjoying a cup of coffee at a seaside café in Bali. Location freedom and travel can open up a world of options for your retirement.

Techniques for Travel and Location Independence:

Make a travel wish list by starting with the places and activities you want to explore during your retirement. Your list will act as a travel compass for anything from historical places to tropical paradises.

Travel expenditures should be factored into your retirement budget. Think of things like travel expenses, lodging, food, and activities. You may travel carefree if you have a special trip fund set aside.

Longer Stays: Instead of short vacations, think about staying longer in various locations. You may fully immerse yourself in the community by renting a vacation house or apartment for a few months.

Explore the lifestyle of a digital nomad if your job or freelancing gigs are location-independent. With an internet connection, you may work from any location while taking in a new environment.

Travel hacking: Master the technique to maximize benefits and savings. Cost-saving travel options include credit card points, frequent flyer miles, and loyalty programs.

Invest in thorough travel insurance to safeguard against unforeseen circumstances like trip cancellations, medical problems, or misplaced luggage.

Plan Ahead: Get arranging for your retirement vacations as soon as possible. To get the lowest prices, plan your trips, make itineraries, and reserve your lodging early.

Acknowledging location independence

Choosing where you wish to live and work is referred to as location independence. It's about eschewing geographical restrictions and leading a life of your choosing.

Location freedom and travel may be an exciting and gratifying feature of your early retirement, whether you want to tour the world as a retiree, immerse yourself in other cultures, or simply spend a portion of the year in your favorite locations. Therefore, begin planning your future travels, pack your spirit of adventure, and let the world be your oyster after you retire!

5.3 Following Your Hobbies And Passions

Welcome to the realm of leisure and fulfillment, where enjoying your interests and passions is the main focus of your early retirement. It's like creating a work of delight out of your idle time!

Why Continue Your Hobbies and Passions After Retirement?

Retirement is about embracing what actually makes you happy and content, not merely giving up employment. Your interests and passions hold the secret to a fulfilling retirement.

As an illustration, picture yourself painting vivid landscapes, jamming with pals, or stargazing as you explore the wonders of the cosmos. Your innermost interests can find a canvas in retirement.

How to Follow Your Passions and Hobbies:

Identify Your Passions: Consider the pursuits and pursuits that give you life. Decide what makes you happy, whether it's gardening, photography, cooking, or collecting rare coins.

Make a budget just for your hobbies by setting aside a percentage of your retirement funds for this purpose. This makes sure you have all you need to take full use of them.

Join Groups or Clubs: Look for groups or clubs in your area that share your interests. Meeting others who share your interests might improve your pastime and lead to new connections.

Learn and Grow: To expand your knowledge and abilities in your chosen pastime, think about enrolling in seminars or workshops. Your retirement endeavors may become more exciting if you learn new methods or strategies.

Establish objectives that are in line with your passions. Setting objectives may help with motivation and a sense of accomplishment, whether it's for cultivating prize-winning roses, finishing a series of paintings, or learning a new musical instrument.

Maintain a Balance: While engaging in your interests is important, do it in moderation. Don't overcommit to the point that you disregard your relationships, health, or financial obligations.

If you have a passion, think about sharing it with others. Create an online instructional, a blog, or a class. Sharing your expertise may be satisfying and even profitable.

5.4 Getting The Most Out Of Retirement:

Your interests and passions are what will keep you busy in retirement. They are the pursuits that give each day enjoyment and significance. Your retirement will be a voyage of self-discovery, creativity, and enjoyment if you invest time and money in what you love.

Your passions and hobbies are your unique invitation to a retirement full of joy and fulfillment, whether you decide to explore a new interest you never had time for, rekindle a long-lost activity, or pursue an artistic gift. Follow your passions, engage in your hobbies, and let the soundtrack of your early retirement be the pursuit of your passions.

Why Should You Strike a Balance Between

Leisure and Productivity in Retirement?

Finding a balance that enables you to take advantage of your newfound freedom while remaining active and content is key to a fulfilling retirement. Your retirement years will have more structure and meaning if you can balance pleasure and productivity.

Consider spending your mornings working at a neighborhood charity and your afternoons reading, drawing, or going on long walks. Your retirement years will be pleasurable and purposeful thanks to this harmony.

Techniques for Juggling Recreation and Productivity:

Set objectives: Establish both leisure- and productivity-focused retirement objectives. What do you hope to accomplish in terms of personal development, societal contribution, or hobbies and interests?

Establish a Schedule: Create a flexible daily or weekly plan that combines productive work with a variety of leisure activities. You can stay organized and motivated by having a schedule.

Give Back by helping: Think about helping for issues you're passionate about. Giving back to the community may be quite gratifying and give your retirement a sense of direction.

Lifelong Learning: Take part in classes, workshops, or online courses to further your education. Maintaining mental acuity and engagement requires stimulating the mind with fresh information and abilities.

Part-time Work or Consulting: Look for part-time employment or consulting options if you like your job or have significant talents. This might boost your retirement income and give you a feeling of success.

Physical activity: Include regular exercise in your daily routine. Staying active, whether via yoga, hiking, or dancing, improves your wellbeing in general.

Keep up your social ties by cultivating new ones. Your retirement experience is enhanced by spending time with loved ones and those who share similar interests.

Don't forget to schedule time for relaxation and self-care. Enjoy the little things in life, whether it's sipping tea, seeing a sunset, or engaging in mindfulness.

Obtaining Balance

Embracing the dualities of retirement—the freedom to unwind and explore new horizons as well as engaging in pursuits that give one a feeling of purpose and accomplishment—is the key to striking a balance between leisure and productivity.

You have the chance to combine production and pleasure in your early retirement in a way that is specially suited to your needs and goals. You may create a retirement lifestyle that is not only pleasurable but also profoundly gratifying by striking this balance. Therefore, let the symphony of productivity and relaxation serve as the music for your senior years as you dance to the beat of your own retirement tune.

CHAPTER 6: NAVIGATING EARLY RETIREMENT CHALLENGES

6.1 Dealing With Unforeseen Expenses

Why Should You Plan for Unexpected Costs?

Unexpected costs are an unfortunate reality of life, and they don't take a holiday when you retire. You may avoid having your goals derailed by being ready for unforeseen financial difficulties.

Imagine your perfect retirement is well underway when a medical emergency or significant house maintenance is discovered. During these times, having a plan in place for unforeseen costs may be relaxing.

Approaches to Deal with Unexpected Expenses:

Maintain an emergency fund that is well filled with at least three to six months' worth of living costs. This reserve fund helps pay for unforeseen expenses without taking money out of your retirement account.

Make sure you have complete insurance protection, such as liability, health, and house insurance. Check your insurance on a regular basis to make sure they still suit your needs.

Flexibility in the Budget: Plan a flexible retirement budget that takes unanticipated expenses into consideration. To avoid being caught off guard, set aside some money in your budget for unforeseen costs.

Prioritize Savings: Even in retirement, prioritize saving. Your emergency fund may be replenished and unplanned expenses can be paid for by setting away a percentage of your retirement income for savings.

Access to Credit: Keep an emergency credit line handy, such as a home equity line of credit (HELOC) or a low-interest credit card. When everything else fails, use these choices with caution.

Keep Up-to-Date: Keep up-to-date on any hazards or difficulties that might arise after retirement. To make sure you're prepared, go to financial planning courses or speak with a financial professional.

Regular Financial Checkups: Review your financial strategy on a regular basis to gauge your readiness for unanticipated costs. To protect your financial stability, modify as required.

Retirement Mental Health:

Even though unexpected costs may not always be preventable, having a proactive financial strategy in place may help you lessen their impact. Your early retirement should be a time of fulfillment and fun, not perpetual stress over unforeseen expenses.

By using these tactics, you're giving yourself the capacity to deal with unanticipated costs with assurance, ensuring that your retirement journey is as easy and pleasurable as possible. Face these unforeseen financial circumstances head-on and allow your early retirement to remain a happy and contented period.

6.2 Managing Health And Healthcare Costs

Why Should Early Retirement Focus on Health and Healthcare Costs?

Your health is your most precious possession, therefore it's crucial to keep it as you approach retirement. Furthermore, controlling healthcare expenses well is essential since they can have a substantial influence on your retirement budget.

Consider the following scenario: You're enjoying your early retirement until a health condition arises that calls for significant medical care. It becomes crucial to control healthcare expenditures if you want to maintain your financial stability.

Techniques for Controlling Health and Medical Costs:

Health Insurance: Sign up for a complete health insurance plan that covers medical costs. Examine alternatives like COBRA or healthcare markets if you are not yet qualified for Medicare.

Plan your transition to Medicare when you are eligible by becoming familiar with the Medicare system. Choosing the best Medicare Advantage or Supplement plan may be necessary in this situation.

Consider purchasing long-term care insurance to help pay for the expenses of nursing homes, assisted living facilities, or in-home care, which may be quite expensive.

Regular Checkups: Make preventative care and regular health checks a priority to identify any problems early and lower the probability of needing expensive medical procedures in the future.

Maintaining a healthy lifestyle involves managing stress, getting enough sleep, and eating right. A healthy lifestyle can lessen the chance of developing chronic diseases and cut down on medical expenses.

Consider using generic medications, mail-order pharmacies, or prescription discount programs to reduce the cost of your prescription medications.

Health Savings Accounts (HSAs): If you qualify, fund an HSA to save money tax-free for medical expenses. HSAs may be a useful tool for controlling medical expenses.

Health care spending should be factored into your retirement budget. This should pay for any projected medical costs as well as insurance premiums, deductibles, and copayments.

Maintain an emergency fund exclusively for situations requiring medical attention. This can assist in paying for unforeseen medical expenses without reducing your retirement resources.

Setting Your Health First:

Early retirement places a premium on health and healthcare expenditures. A proactive approach to maintaining health and controlling medical costs may protect your financial stability in addition to your physical wellbeing.

You are taking the essential actions to negotiate the difficulties of healthcare in retirement by adhering to these techniques. Make preserving your health a top priority since it will improve your retirement quality of life. Make your retirement a time of vigor, happiness, and financial security.

6.3 Maintaining A Social Network

Why Stay Connected to Social Media in Early Retirement?

Maintaining a social network becomes essential when you enter retirement for a number of reasons. It lessens loneliness, offers emotional support, and improves the general standard of your retirement years.

Take early retirement as an example, but without a social network. Your general wellbeing might be impacted by loneliness, which can creep in and cause emptiness-related symptoms.

Methods for Keeping a Social Network Active:

Maintain Contact: Try to keep in touch with your friends and family. If feasible, schedule regular phone conversations, video conferences, or in-person meetings.

Join Groups or Clubs: Get involved in clubs, organizations, or hobbyist associations that share your interests. This offers chances to connect with others who share your interests and start new connections.

Volunteer: Think about giving your time to issues you find important. You can meet new people while volunteering, and it also provides you a feeling of fulfillment and purpose.

Attend Social Events: Participate in social gatherings, events, and neighborhood activities. These present chances for socializing and enlarging your social network.

Join online forums and groups that are relevant to your interests or hobbies. Connections made virtually can be just as valuable as those made in person.

Take seminars or workshops in subjects that interest you to learn something new. Social connection chances are facilitated through group learning.

Travel with Company: If you want to travel, think about going on a tour with friends or a group. Togetherness may be strengthened through traveling to new areas.

Mentorship: Provide advice and guidance to others, especially if you have relevant information or skills to impart.

Maintain Existing Relationships: Keep in mind your current relationships. Reach out to one another and arrange to spend time together to foster these relationships.

Accepting Social Relationships:

In order to invest in your mental wellbeing and foster a sense of belonging, maintaining a social network during early retirement is important. Although sound financial preparation is important, developing and maintaining strong connections can make your retirement richer.

You can make sure your retirement years are full with meaningful contacts, shared experiences, and a feeling of community by using these tactics. Make your social network the tapestry that adds joy, laughter, and a feeling of community to your early retirement.

6.4 Staying Engaged And Fulfilled

Welcome to the big finale of early retirement knowledge, where we discuss how to maintain a sense of purpose and engagement throughout this thrilling phase of your life. It's similar like leading a passionate, purposeful orchestra.

Why Put an Emphasis on Staying Engaged and Content in Early Retirement?

Early retirement is about enjoying a life that still excites and fulfills you, not just ceasing employment. Retirement stays an adventure rather than a plateau by maintaining your sense of purpose.

Consider the following scenario: You have retired early but lack a sense of direction or hobbies that thrill you. Days might seem pointless, and retirement starts to lose its appeal.

Strategies for Remaining Involved and Content

Set meaningful objectives first: Establish worthwhile objectives that reflect your values and interests. These objectives may be private, professional, or centered around interests and passions.

2. Embrace Lifelong Learning: Develop an open mind and keep learning even after you retire. Take classes, read, or investigate new topics and abilities.

3. Travel and Exploration: To satiate your curiosity and spirit of adventure, visit new places locally or abroad.

4. Creative Expression: Take part in activities that are enjoyable for you, such as writing, singing, or other forms of artistic expression.

5. Physical Health: Give your physical health first priority by being active through exercise, yoga, or other enjoyable physical pursuits.

6. *Mindfulness:* Be mindful of your mental well-being. Therapy or mindfulness-based techniques can support emotional well-being.

7. *Engage with Other:* Continue to socialize socially, volunteer, or mentor with others. For happiness, a connection to other people is necessary.

8. *Give Back:* Think of ways to support your neighborhood or a cause you care deeply about. Making a difference for something bigger than yourself may be quite satisfying.

9. *Balanced Lifestyle:* Maintain a healthy balance between leisure time and work. Balance makes ensuring you're neither overburdened nor immobile.

10. *Celebrate Achievements:* Honor your accomplishments, whether significant and minor. Your sense of contentment may increase if you acknowledge your development and accomplishments.

Living a Meaningful Retirement:

An opportunity to live life on your terms, with passion, purpose, and excitement, is early retirement. It's about pursuing your passions and carrying on your journey of development, education, and exploration.

By employing these tactics, you can make sure that your golden years are a celebration of all the things that make you happy and content. Let your early retirement serve as the blank canvas for you to create a work of art that is meaningful and engaging.

Throughout this great trip, may every day be an adventure and your sense of fulfillment serve as the soundtrack.

EPILOGUE

The Journey Continues

Remember that the conclusion of this book is only the beginning of a new chapter in your life—a thrilling chapter of financial freedom, personal growth, and realizing your dreams—as we draw to a close our voyage through the pages of "Rat Race No More: How to Retire Early and Live Your Dreams."

You have arrived at the freeing beaches of early retirement from the never-ending grind of the rat race. You've learned the value of sound financial planning along the way, as well as the fun of pursuing your interests and the satisfaction of leaving a lasting legacy. Your path has served as evidence of your tenacity, fortitude, and unrelenting dedication to live life on your terms.

The tale of adventure, self-discovery, and continual dream quest continues; the story does not finish here. Your retirement is a blank canvas that is just waiting to be painted with the vivid strokes of your passions, the brush of your knowledge, and the colours of your ideals.

As you begin this new chapter, keep in mind to:

Consider Your Journey: Take some time to reflect on your accomplishments and the vast distance you've traveled. Each step has been a victory, whether it was getting your finances in order, following your interests, or leaving a lasting legacy.

Embrace the Future: Retirement is an adventure filled with limitless opportunities. Continue to create objectives, be true to your ideals, and be open to new experiences. Your goals are limitless, and your ambitions are always changing.

Encourage Others: Inform individuals around you about your experiences and advice. Be a source of inspiration and knowledge for people who want to leave the grind and become financially independent. Positive changes in people's lives may be a result of your trip.

Leave a Lasting Legacy: Your legacy will be one of empowerment, freedom, and opportunity. Continue to have a good effect on the world, whether via giving, mentoring, or just by inspiring others.

Your path from the rat race to early retirement is a magnificent thread that runs through the tales of many other people who have the courage to dream in the big fabric of life. Your legacy includes not just the things you leave behind but also the people you affect, the hopes and aspirations you foster, and the lives you touch.

You have the pleasure and duty to write a life that has meaning, joy, and satisfaction because you are the author of your own tale. I hope your next travels are just as exciting and fulfilling as those that got you here.

Consequently, when we say goodbye to these pages, keep in mind that your retirement is a blank canvas just waiting for your masterpiece—a colorful, constantly-evolving piece of art that represents the hues of your aspirations and the curves of your heart's wishes.

The most amazing part of the voyage is yet to come.

With sincere hopes for a future brimming with limitless opportunities,

~Mohd Faisal

ABOUT THE AUTHOR

Mohd Faisal

Mohd Faisal as an Indian author has penned several motivational books such as "The Ikigai Blueprints", "39 Commandments for Financial Success", and "Dark Triad Unmasked" etc. His books have helped thousands of readers across the globe to take control of their lives and achieve their dreams. His books offer practical advice and  actionable strategies for overcoming obstacles and achieving success in all areas of life.

BOOKS BY THIS AUTHOR

The Ikigai Blueprint : The Secrets To Financial Freedom For A Rich And Fulfilling Life.

"The Ikigai Blueprint: For A Rich And Fulfilling Life" is a guidebook that delves into the Japanese concept of Ikigai and provides a roadmap for finding purpose and fulfillment in life.
Based on the teachings of the Japanese island of Okinawa, the book explores the four key elements of Ikigai - what you love, what you are good at, what the world needs, and what you can be paid for - and shows how these elements can be combined to create a fulfilling life.

The book combines practical advice, inspiring stories, and thought-provoking exercises to help readers find their own personal Ikigai and live a life filled with joy, purpose, and meaning. Whether you are seeking to improve your career, deepen your relationships, or simply live a more fulfilling life, "The Ikigai Blueprint" provides a blueprint for creating a life of abundance, happiness, and purpose.

Money Paradox: Balancing Money, Greed, And Contentment

"Money Paradox" takes you on a fascinating voyage of self-discovery and introspection in a world dominated by the desire of riches and the attraction of materialism. Discover the keys to creating a life of meaning, satisfaction, and enduring joy by delving into the complex dance of money, wants, and contentment.

Why You Should Try This Book:
Explore the intricate link between wealth and happiness from a novel perspective by examining the psychological factors, cultural standards, and personal beliefs that shape our financial choices.
Gaining effective ideas can help you strike a healthy balance between your monetary objectives and your inner satisfaction. Learn how to embrace mindful consumption, create meaningful connections, and match your financial decisions with your ideals.
Real-existence Stories: Set off on an engrossing journey via the experiences of people who have faced the money dilemma and discovered their way to a more fulfilling and well-balanced existence.
Mindful Reflections: Take part in introspective activities and reflective reflections that challenge you to think critically about your personal relationship with money and open the door to transformational change.
Holistic Approach: Unlike conventional finance publications, "Money Paradox" offers a holistic approach on financial well-being by delving into the emotional, psychological, and spiritual elements of money in addition to providing budgeting guidance.
Discover timeless truths that endure through passing fads and provide a solid framework for addressing the challenges of contemporary life.

What Makes This Book Unique:
Interdisciplinary Exploration: To give a thorough understanding of the complex interactions between money and satisfaction, the book skillfully weaves together concepts from psychology, philosophy, and personal development.
Narrative Depth: "Money Paradox" is more than simply a how-to manual; it's a narrative journey that captures your heart and intellect and enables you to relate to people's challenges and victories as they seek balance.

Practical and Philosophical: The book equips you to make wise financial decisions while asking you to reflect on the more profound issues of purpose and meaning. It does this by balancing philosophical reflection with practical counsel.

A balanced reading experience that fosters both personal development and practical application is provided through each chapter's tangible instructions and thought-provoking comments.

While the book is grounded in the present, its concepts and insights are timeless, making it a useful tool for anybody looking for permanent contentment in a constantly shifting environment.

The transformative guide "Money Paradox: Balancing Money, Greed, and Contentment" is more than simply a book; it equips you with the knowledge, intention, and fresh sense of purpose needed to successfully negotiate the intricacies of riches, wants, and well-being. Set off on this adventure right now to find the secrets to a life of true fulfillment and permanent joy.

Money Magnet Mantras: A Step-By-Step Guide To Making And Retaining Money

Uncover the Wealth and Abundance Secrets!

Are you fed up with continuously battling your finances? Are you ready to escape the cycle of scarcity and enter a world of abundance? There is no need to look any further! The book "Money Magnet Mantras: A Step-by-Step Guide to Making and Retaining Money" is here to change your financial fate!

Discover the Secrets of Money Magnetism

This game-changing book has the key to uncovering the hidden secrets of attracting and preserving riches. It unravels the intricacies of building a mentality that naturally attracts money in a step-by-step method, while also giving you with practical techniques to make it work in your advantage.

Unlock Your Financial Potential

Inside "Money Magnet Mantras," you'll go on a life-changing trip in which you'll discover how to:
Retrain your mind to think in terms of abundance.
Discover the underlying beliefs that are holding you back.
Use affirmations and imagery to your advantage.
Master the art of money manifestation.
Create long-term wealth-building behaviors
Create a long-term asset preservation strategy.
Empower Yourself, Change Your Life

This is not your typical financial handbook; it is a game-changing manual that will empower you to take charge of your financial destiny. "Money Magnet Mantras," written by recognized financial professionals and supported by substantial research, provides a road map to financial independence unlike any other.

Don't Pass Up This Golden Opportunity!

Take advantage of this opportunity to change your relationship with money and build a wealthy future. Ignite the power of riches inside yourself and create the life you've always desired! Order your copy of "Money Magnet Mantras" immediately to take advantage of our limited-time promotion!

Activate Your Wealth Potential Today!

Money Paradox: Balancing Money, Greed, And

Contentment

"Money Paradox" takes you on a fascinating voyage of self-discovery and introspection in a world dominated by the desire of riches and the attraction of materialism. Discover the keys to creating a life of meaning, satisfaction, and enduring joy by delving into the complex dance of money, wants, and contentment.

Why You Should Try This Book:
Explore the intricate link between wealth and happiness from a novel perspective by examining the psychological factors, cultural standards, and personal beliefs that shape our financial choices.
Gaining effective ideas can help you strike a healthy balance between your monetary objectives and your inner satisfaction. Learn how to embrace mindful consumption, create meaningful connections, and match your financial decisions with your ideals.
Real-existence Stories: Set off on an engrossing journey via the experiences of people who have faced the money dilemma and discovered their way to a more fulfilling and well-balanced existence.
Mindful Reflections: Take part in introspective activities and reflective reflections that challenge you to think critically about your personal relationship with money and open the door to transformational change.
Holistic Approach: Unlike conventional finance publications, "Money Paradox" offers a holistic approach on financial well-being by delving into the emotional, psychological, and spiritual elements of money in addition to providing budgeting guidance.
Discover timeless truths that endure through passing fads and provide a solid framework for addressing the challenges of contemporary life.

What Makes This Book Unique:
Interdisciplinary Exploration: To give a thorough understanding of the complex interactions between money and satisfaction, the

book skillfully weaves together concepts from psychology, philosophy, and personal development.

Narrative Depth: "Money Paradox" is more than simply a how-to manual; it's a narrative journey that captures your heart and intellect and enables you to relate to people's challenges and victories as they seek balance.

Practical and Philosophical: The book equips you to make wise financial decisions while asking you to reflect on the more profound issues of purpose and meaning. It does this by balancing philosophical reflection with practical counsel.

A balanced reading experience that fosters both personal development and practical application is provided through each chapter's tangible instructions and thought-provoking comments.

While the book is grounded in the present, its concepts and insights are timeless, making it a useful tool for anybody looking for permanent contentment in a constantly shifting environment.

The transformative guide "Money Paradox: Balancing Money, Greed, and Contentment" is more than simply a book; it equips you with the knowledge, intention, and fresh sense of purpose needed to successfully negotiate the intricacies of riches, wants, and well-being. Set off on this adventure right now to find the secrets to a life of true fulfillment and permanent joy.

The Manifestation Mantras: Boost Your Manifestation Power Through Indian Vedic And Sufi Practices.

Are you struggling to manifest your goals and desires in life? Do you feel like you're constantly hitting roadblocks and setbacks? If so, "Manifestation Mantras" is the book for you!

Drawing on the powerful practices of Indian Vedic and Sufi traditions, this book offers a unique and transformative approach to manifestation. With the help of ancient mantras and affirmations, you'll learn how to tap into the limitless power of the universe and align yourself with your deepest desires.

Whether you're looking to attract abundance, find love, or achieve career success, "Manifestation Mantras" will guide you on your journey. You'll discover practical techniques for harnessing the power of intention, visualizing your dreams, and staying focused on your goals. With each chapter, you'll gain a deeper understanding of yourself and the world around you, and develop the skills you need to create a life of joy and fulfillment.

With its insightful teachings and inspiring guidance, "Manifestation Mantras" is a must-read for anyone looking to unlock their full potential and manifest their dreams into reality. So why wait? Start your journey of transformation today!

Permaculture Mantras: The Wisdom Of Ancient Indian Permaculture

Are you prepared to set out on a transforming adventure and discover the permaculture secrets of prehistoric India? Introducing the fascinating book "Permaculture Mantras: The Wisdom of Ancient Indian Permaculture," which will direct you toward a sustainable and regenerative way of life.

Discover the strength of permaculture ideas rooted in the rich tradition of ancient India in this enlightening and inspirational book. Explore the interconnectivity of nature, the significance of ethical behavior, and the significant effects these things may have on our lives and the globe as we delve into the depths of wisdom that has been passed down through the decades.

This book is an all-inclusive guide to living in harmony with nature, covering everything from creating a permaculture garden to putting sustainable energy solutions into practice. It is written in a conversational and engaging tone, with compelling tales and thought-provoking quotes that permeate each chapter. The author's sarcastic writing style serves as an inspiration as they guide readers through the complexities of permaculture principles.

Whether you're a seasoned permaculturist or someone new with an inquisitive mind, "Permaculture Mantras" will lead you on an illuminating trip and provide you the skills and knowledge you need to have a positive influence. It's time to get back in touch with nature, practice sustainability, and live a more regenerative lifestyle.

Join the struggle for a future that is greener and more peaceful. Immerse yourself in the permaculture knowledge of the ancient Indians, and let it direct your every move. Purchase a copy of "Permaculture Mantras: The Wisdom of Ancient Indian Permaculture" right away to begin your journey toward change and a life where sustainability is the norm.

~ THE END ~